If God Invented Baseball

Poems by

E. ETHELBERT MILLER

City Point Press

City Point Press

PO Box 2063

Westport CT 06880

www.citypointpress.com

Paperback ISBN: 978-1-947951-00-6

eBook ISBN: 978-1-947951-01-3

Third printing, February 2024

Cover design by Barbara Aronica-Buck

Author photo © 2017 Rick Reinhard

Cover photo of Satchel Paige, courtesy of the Baseball Hall of Fame

Writing was a curveball that I never saw coming.

– Larry Brown

Becoming a baseball fan means learning to absorb
failure and be on a friendly footing with defeat.

– Phillip Lopate

Baseball is the greatest of American games.

– Thomas Edison

Contents

Preface

When I was growing up in the South Bronx baseball was the game I played across the street. It was in the playground next to P.S. 39. I lived at 938 Longwood Avenue on the second floor. A cousin Robert lived two floors above and possessed the name Dinky. He was two years older but ahead of his time. Dinky read books by Herman Khan, Isaac Asimov and Arthur C. Clarke.

He also loved Roberto Clemente, Tommy Davis and Don Drysdale. Dinky and I would play baseball together even when there was snow on the ground.

There is no future without baseball. There is no past either. My childhood memories will always embrace the New York Yankees of Bobby Richardson, Tony Kubek, Bill Skowron, Roger Maris, Mickey Mantle, Yogi Berra, Hector Lopez and Elston Howard. Yes, a line-up of remembrance.

The idea for *If God Invented Baseball* came from David Wilk. Our mutual love of the game encouraged the writing of many of these poems.

Thanks has to be given to the people responsible for bringing baseball back to our nation's capital. One should always have a romantic relationship with a sports team. I love the Washington Nationals with all the joy and heartbreak only a Cubs or Red Sox fan would understand.

I admire Dusty Baker and should have written this book with a toothpick in my mouth.

Here are poems that celebrate and interpret the game. They are for everyone who has experienced the magic released when three holy things come together: bat, ball and glove.

E. Ethelbert Miller
Blue Mountain Center, New York
July 22, 2017

Before Ball Four

It was the summer

we wanted our caps

to fall from our heads.

I stood on line

outside Yankee Stadium

waiting for Jim Bouton

to sign my glove.

Bouton was a pitcher

not a writer then. I was a kid

who wanted to be a ball player.

It was years before

I knew the difference

between writing and throwing

or pitching and publishing.

If God Invented Baseball

If God invented baseball
There would be no stealing
no balks, no wild pitches or intentional
walks. There would be no pitch-outs,
foul balls or errors. There would be
no one-hand catches or bean balls.
There would be no curves or sliders,
no rundowns, or warning tracks.

If God invented baseball there would
be no night games, no balls getting lost
in the sun. There would be no bunting
or swinging for the fences. There would
be no double plays or triple plays.

If God invented baseball
he would not rest on the seventh day.
Instead he would turn to us and say
"let's play two." He would let us bat
first while his angels danced
in the outfield.

The South Bronx

We lived in the land of broomsticks

stickball played between cars

manholes for bases

We ran pass fire hydrants

and caught balls near curbs

Now and then someone smacked

a Spaldeen to a rooftop-

Making pigeons fly

Baseball Is An Island Not A Field

(for Martín Espada)

No one mentioned the Dominican Republic
when I was growing up. We were all Puerto
Ricans. We were little baby bulls like Orlando
Cepeda.

Playing Until Dark

When we could no longer see

the ball we walked home sadly

dragging our bats and sometimes

wearing our gloves on our heads.

Exhausted but happy.

The light in our eyes

even stars could see.

Fences

In the playgrounds

there were few left-handed

hitters so right field

is where the big kids placed us.

We became ghosts of the game.

We stood alone in sunlight.

Sometimes during a third out

we escaped through a hole in the fence.

We returned home like players sent down

to the minors.

Juan, Willie and The Boys

In the park we high-kicked

before throwing the ball.

We wanted to be Marichal

more than Mays – unless

we were running around

the bases. Then we wanted

our caps to fly off giving us

the speed the big boys

didn't have. Reaching home

we were safe.

The backs of our arms

covered with dust. Our good

shirts torn but everyone laughing —

fall down silly.

Players

When Mickey Mantle died

I saw myself once again

jumping against a fence

in the South Bronx, the ball

coming to rest in my glove.

My own centerfield as large

as the housing projects

so many could not escape.

Judy

From 4th to 6th grade
The back corners of my school
desks were filled with love notes
from Judy.

We practiced penmanship
as much as we played catch.

Judy was my first love
and we were married to baseball
even if we were too young to go
steady.

Judy was Chinese. After our first
kiss we traded gloves.

The Boys of Summer

Carlton, Patrick and I

are waiting for autographs

outside Yankee Stadium. The summer

of 1960 and Mazeroski has not hit

the home run which will break our

hearts. We are years away from

memories of our wives and our children.

On this day we see Mickey Mantle coming

to work, his uniform of stripes waiting

inside. We run to catch "The Mick" to

have him sign his name on whatever we

own. Our lives sheltered from segregation.

Our mothers talking about Jackie Robinson

and how Willie Mays learned to catch a ball

while turning his back, running full speed

as if he were Emmett Till.

The Walkoff

Our games ended

when the ball was lost.

Now and then a hit over a fence

rolled down the street into the sewer.

We blamed each other and ourselves.

We were kids caught in a playground

pushing our imaginations

to imagine ballparks.

This was years before last inning

heroics and bat flips. Men now paint

with wood, standing back admiring

the flight of their art. What is

the difference between a fence

and a frame?

Bunting and The Art of Non-Violence

All your life you played small ball.
In elementary school you held the door
open for your teacher. This taught you
the art of bunting and kind manners.

You sacrificed being first so someone
could reach second. Once returning
to the dugout Gandhi slapped your butt
and said "good job."

He also said "the bat is not a club."

One Man's Fast Is Another Man's Slow

Since I never learned to drive

I never called my legs wheels.

During my Bronx days

I was fast. I could catch. I could hit.

I could run.

I was captain. I could pick

My team. No slow boys. No

Over eaters.

I wanted legs like Luis Aparicio,

Willie Davis, Maury Wills

And Lou Brock.

Oh, let me write words from another book

Pinch hit and walk off the page.

Let them mention Ricky Henderson.

Everything comes down to balls and strikes.

You don't need religion or God to understand this.

One can keep a scorecard just like God. Now and then you

try to slow things down by stepping out of the box.

I like how good hitters step back, adjust their uniforms,

stroke their bats, survey the field, spit, grab themselves

between the legs, step back into the box, touch their

caps, stare at the pitcher, swing the bat a few times,

and maybe if you're Rickey Henderson, step back out

of the box and do it all over again.

High School and The Intentional Walk

My guidance counselor

Sits behind a desk with catalogs

and big books. Her office is near

the bathroom and the broom

closet where the custodian

keeps his clean clothes and lunch.

Going to see the counselor

is worse than being sent to the main

office. In the office the old women

wear short skirts and still smile.

The guidance counselor has never

guided her face to a smile. She

is as serious as bad cafeteria food

on a Monday.

Today she wants to know

what I plan to do with my life.

She asks if I've selected a career.

She keeps asking me what I want

to do with my life. She asks if I've

selected a career. I keep listening

to her the way a manager talks

to a starting pitcher before removing him

from a game. I'm nodding and he's nodding

and I'm not listening.

My guidance counselor

extends her hand letting me know

our meeting is over. I notice her desk

sits in the middle of the room like a mound.

There is nothing but emptiness behind

every decision we make in life.

Yes, maybe I'm throwing my life away.

Maybe she's trying too hard to help.

All I know is that I'm walking out the door

and I'm out of control. I can't read the signs

anymore. I'm a high school kid knowing

I'll never see the majors or Japan.

The Trade

Your parents call you

into their bedroom. They've

been whispering and your ears

want to hear what they hear but you

fear what it might be. Your mom

speaks first because your dad always

speaks second. You fear they both

are trying to teach you how to chew

your food, wash your hands, tuck

your shirt and tie your shoes.

Everything is unexpected like a baseball

trade. Your mom says you're going

to a new school and it's the one across

town, the place where the white kids are.

You look down at your skin and notice

for the first time you're black. You never

wore a different uniform. You've been black

all your life. You wouldn't change this for all

the blackness in the world. You wouldn't change

it for all the whiteness now.

You give your mom a Curt Flood look

and your dad nothing at all. You turn

from the doorway and walk back

to your room. You feel traded. You feel

betrayed.

Outside your window

the birds are chirping blues.

Ma Rainey is singing about the Mississippi risin'.

Sam Cooke calls from next door and says

"Yes, a flood is comin' and a change is gonna

come."

Holy Water

It's raining today and nothing else matters.

When I was an altar boy I wanted to be Clete Boyer.

I lived on Longwood Avenue in the Bronx.

The hot corner was Kelly Street and it was hell hot.

Yankee Stadium was heaven.

Nothing more beautiful than Boyer

throwing a runner out from his knees.

War Catchers

Once only catchers wore

their caps backwards.

Was the face mask an

introduction to prison?

You either wanted to catch

or you didn't. Catchers

walked around with bruises

and scars. Many were short

and tough. They were

veterans who sat on the bench

and told war stories about

extra inning games and no-hit

gems. Catchers turned their

caps backwards while slow-

walking to the plate. They

nodded to umpires and spoke

only to the game.

The Bat Boy

The sound of ball against bone

was still in my head when I went

to get Gil McDougald's bat.

The park as silent as a cemetery.

The body of Herb Score cut down

at the mound and lying limp –

did the world end on May 7, 1957?

It was the day McDougald vowed

to never play again if Score lost

his right eye. I told my mom

that night I didn't want to see

another bat or ball. I had a fear

of seeing blindness and knowing

stars could disappear.

The Second Child

(for Nyere-Gibran)

in sports they say it's difficult

to repeat, to win, to gain a championship

two consecutive years; so it is with children,

the difference, the new season, the second child.

Each beginning finds a newborn, a rookie

struggling to learn the lessons of spring,

a time of hope and expectations, of fingers

gripping and pulling things to mouth.

The Utility Infielder

My wife without telling me

moves my books out of the basement.

I'm Tony Kubek watching the ball

take a bad bounce as it grabs my throat.

It's the 7th game of the World Series –

Yankees against Pirates.

In 1960 my wife had yet to speak

to me. We didn't even know each other.

Did Joe DeMaestri ever date or just play

every position?

I am Tony Kubek

unable to explain my life.

Long ago it was DeMaestri's baseball card

I wanted to give away. What worth

would it ever have?

Marriage is the sweet pink chewing gum

that comes with the cards. It loses

its taste before we blow and pop

that first bubble, before we divorce

or try to outrun the errors of our love.

The Knuckleball

Every black man should be born
with a big mitt.
How else can one catch the world
that flutters in unpredictable ways.

The sound of a knuckleball
is Parker on his horn.
When Ella scats don't try
to copy her.

Oriole Hoyt Wilhelm in 1958 threw
a no-hitter against the Yankees.
It was like Douglass being Lincoln
for a day. It's impossible to dance
to slavery anymore. It ended with
the hangman's swing.

The knuckleball is Bebop.
Don't be baffled by its strange beauty.
Just keep hitting it with your ears.

The Throw

Before darkness descended
Lightning came from right field.

Kaline, Clemente and Rocky Colavito
Threw like Gods.

No runner or sinner could run
Or dash to third.

The ballpark silenced by thunder
Hitting the glove.

Eyes blinded by the beauty
Of the throw.

The Pitch Out

The ball moves

toward

the plate

like a note

played by

Ben Webster

a sound so large

you just listen

as it passes far

outside your ear

You're surprised

when the catcher

catches the ball

he wants to throw

The runner on first

stops

in his tracks

like a young jazz critic

Why run?

Crosetti

Frank Crosetti

a gentleman in pinstripes

stands near third base.

How many heroes

will he escort home?

1932 and Ruth looks into

the Cubs dugout,

points a finger and calls

the shot.

A young Crosetti will think

of the Babe when he shakes

the hand of Roger Maris in

1961.

Baseball is a game played

by men who know the silence

of grace and the beauty of

records made to be broken.

Bill Mazeroski Returns Home From The World Series

when i was a kid

i told my old man

that i would make a name for myself

like walter next door who had a hit

record on the radio for two weeks

and then enlisted and got himself shot

i want people to forget Eisenhower

i want them to remember my swing

the way I touched third and headed

home to every fan in the world

Fly Balls and Other Beautiful Things

Bob Gibson came to Nat Turner in a dream.

He taught him how to freedom pitch and brush back slavery.

A cardinal is a messenger from God.

The arc of a Josh Gibson home run

Was what Harriet Tubman was told to follow.

The voices in her head constantly ran the bases.

Those of us who heard Frederick Douglass

learned to step off first base and get a lead.

He taught us how to avoid the pickoff and rundown.

His hair was filled with beautiful things.

Moe Berg

What man doesn't have secrets?

What man doesn't wear a mask?

Every catcher hides his signs

from the man on second

and from the rest of the world.

If Moe Berg was a spy

he was our spy

protecting home.

Behind every catcher

only a lonely umpire

calling the game like God.

The First Man. Was Vic Power Created Before Adam?

They yell "clown" from the dugout and stands.

"Showboat" is a foul word in the air like "Nigger."

I swear they should be yelling at Chief Wahoo on my

sleeve and not the Puerto Rican in me.

I ignore the taunts.

Why catch abuse with two hands?

If God invented baseball and wanted everyone

to be like him, why don't we play with two gloves?

Pumpsie Green

Years before we decided to change

our names and name ourselves

I held your baseball card in black

hands and wondered who gave you

the name Pumpsie.

How unforgettable, as if Nat

King Cole had decided to sing your

name. You were the first black player

to play for Boston. I wondered about

the ear's loneliness when you got a

hit or the error someone made when

calling you to bunt and run.

How green was the Fenway field

before your arrival? Your name

a sign against segregation finally

finding a place in the locker room.

Pumpsie Green. What Red Sox
fan mistook your last name for
being Irish after being puzzled
by your first?

Jackie Robinson

After baseball

his hair turned gray

as if someone had placed

a tarp over the field.

Koufax and Me

(for Aviva)

One didn't have to be Jewish

to love Sandy Koufax. With Jackie

Robinson we learned to root for the best bums

in the world.

Equality was captured when he stole a base.

In 1957 the Dodgers left Brooklyn.

Stolen by Los Angeles.

Koufax became a star close to Hollywood.

I was amazed by what he could do with a curve

and how a girl could swing her hips.

I was a sutterer in school.

I was Willie Davis making those errors

in the 1966 World Series.

Roy Campanella: January, 1958

Night as dark as the inside

of a catcher's mitt.

There are blows I can take

head on and never step back

from. When Jackie made the news

I knew I would have a chance

to play ball in the majors.

Ten years ago I put the number

39 on my back and tonight God

tries to steal home.

Vida Blue

Before the band takes

the stage, backstage

everyone is waiting

for Vida Blue. You can't

play the music without

the pitcher or the bass

player.

"Mingus" someone mumbles,

scaring the cigarette smoke

in the corner. "Is he in the dugout

or the underground?"

It's 1971 and Vida Blue

is strumming the mound

for the Oakland A's. Notes

popping in and out of the catcher's

mitt and making the leather sing

like Ella, or is it Vaughan?

I once took the A train

to the park where I saw Blue

Moon Odom and Billy Strayhorn

standing outside the corner of first

and second. Ellington the manager

was looking dapper and had his arm

around a dame.

I swore the woman was

sweet divine and as royal as the Duke.

I was a heckler until the beer knocked

me down and Vida Blue caught me

lookin'.

Barry Bonds

(for Dan Moldea)

Only Shakespeare could write my biography.

My swing was pure Picasso, surreal to the average

player and fan. Forget the Babe.

My name is Bonds. Barry Bonds.

I was blessed by the gods and my godfather

is Willie Mays. Yes, I played for the Giants

and was once a Pirate. Folks try to place a patch

over my records but it only makes them blind

to beauty. Every rumor comes with steroids

and becomes larger with every lie. Leaving

me out of the Hall of Fame makes the place

nothing but a hall. Call me the Ali of baseball.

The greatest of them all.

Japanese Flowers Bloom
Inside A Baseball Bat

Baseball is spoken

in every language.

Ichiro stretches

at bat and in the outfield.

Mariner, Yankee

Marlin.

Every hit

a haiku.

Baseball Blues

Dusty Baker plays his toothpick like a guitar.

A bad bullpen will always give a team the baseball blues.

The 7th Inning Stretch

(for Lynda Tredway)

Let me rise like Lazarus.

Let me bask in the sun with my fellow fans.

Let me sway with the music.

Let me point at the scoreboard and ignore the score.

Let me wave my cap.

Let me open my arms and embrace my last innings.

Let me celebrate baseball.

Let me celebrate life.

The Pitch Count

Is it the 9th inning

when death jogs from the bullpen

to face you in your final at bat?

Or maybe it's spring training

when hope fails like health

and the team heads north

without you.

Blame it on the pitch count

when you slump after the All-Star

game in the middle season of your

life.

Suddenly the fever of August and the first

chill of September followed by knowing

you will not play in October.

There is something final

and not forgiving about the final out.

The ball taken from your hand.

Baseball begins and ends at home.

The Relief Pitcher Throws A Sonnet

You have to forget the last election.

The blown save.

What matters is now, not tomorrow, just now.

In every inning there is the possibility of something going wrong,

the way sunlight blinds or the way a ball skips towards

the wall or through and under a glove. You stand on the mound

of your imagination and imagine nothing except your own breath.

In your hands the roundness of the world.

How do you feel? Is this what you've always wanted?

It's not about the score or getting out of the inning.

It's about saving whatever needs to be saved. It can be nothing

more than one's reputation or helping a child crave the memory

of magic and something to believe in. There is nothing more

human than baseball.

Rain Delay

The rain stops in mid-air

like Satchel Paige throwing

his hesitation pitch or the Supreme

Court deciding it's all deliberate

speed when it comes to integration.

Segregation was America's dark cloud,

a mud stain on white uniforms.

The scoreboard a reminder that waiting

was a wasted turn at bat.

The rain continues to fall in one direction.

Who can say this is progress?

The Playoffs

while i watch the playoffs

you use my phone to call

some other man

you stay until

the fifth inning

then you say you have

to leave

i watch you exit

like a pitcher heading

for the showers

somewhere someone

is keeping score

you perfect your game

with each man

love is the best curve

a woman can throw

Wild Pitch

She throws the pillows to the floor

with hurt and anger. It's difficult to determine

where the plate of love is.

You want to call this home but a divorce

is as good as a walk.

Ice Age After The Game

I remove shoes

Socks and pants.

I reach for the ice

For arms and knees.

How many blocks

Now turn into innings?

I can barely walk.

Is this intentional?

I unbutton my shirt

And stare at the gray

Splinters of hair. I place

The ice everywhere.

In this game

Nothing melts faster

Than age.

The Bullpen

I enter the assisted

living home. Everyday

is Sunday here.

Instead of pews

many sit in wheelchairs.

Our last innings

are when we give thanks

for small things.

Elders are closers.

We turn to them for hope

as they rise and march

into history wearing

crowns, suits and shoes

that shine.

Old Timer's Day

The workers arrived today
bringing tools to change
my home place. My place
one day will no longer be safe.
This is what aging does to
the body, when things fail
and the walls of youth become
Berlin after the cold war.
Old age is coldness, bones
reduced to everything that is
fragile. How we break is how
we suffer, it's how we die,
it's how we dream backwards.

The workers install railings
and handle bars to prevent
my falling as if falling in love
was still possible. I loved the
Yankees when I was young,

when I thought I could be

a pitcher, yes, I wanted my name

to be called on Old-Timer's Day

after all my mistakes and errors.

Call my name God after Jim Coates,

Art Ditmar, Ryne Duren, Whitey

Ford, Don Larsen, Duke Maas, Bobby

Shantz, Ralph Terry, Bob Turley,

Luis Arroyo and tall Steve Hamilton.

Call my name God when I walk

slowly from the dugout to wave

at the crowd, tip my hat and call

it a day.

Baseball

Let me sit in the ball park

cap turned backwards and

praying for a rally. I need

the sun and sweat to remind

me how much I love the game,

how each year it comes down

to the last inning, the final out.

Invention

Across the street Thomas Edison

listens to Bessie Smith and decides

the blues are too painful

for anyone crying alone in the dark.

Seasons

Spring training again

Young players replace the old

The game is too short

The Zen of Baseball

Maybe we should play baseball

by the lake. The motion of water

as still as a pitcher waiting for a sign.

The surrounding trees standing

like coaches and managers.

Who wouldn't want to walk across

the lake into immortality.

About the Author

E. Ethelbert Miller is a writer and literary activist. He is the author of several collections of poems and two memoirs and serves as a board member for the Greater Washington Community Foundation. For fourteen years Miller has been the editor of *Poet Lore,* the oldest poetry magazine published in the United States. In April 2015, Miller was inducted into the Washington DC Hall of Fame. In 2016, he received the AWP *George Garrett Award for Outstanding Community Service in Literature* and the DC Mayor's Arts Award for *Distinguished Honor.* Miller currently serves on the faculty at the University of Houston/Victoria and hosts the weekly morning radio show *On the Margin* which airs on WPFW-FM 89.3. His most recent book is *The Collected Poems of E. Ethelbert Miller* edited by Kirsten Porter and published by Willow Books.